Christmas Cracker Joke Book

Ha! Ha!

www.booksbyboxer.com

Published in the UK by
Books By Boxer, Leeds, LS13 4BS
© Books By Boxer 2014
All Rights Reserved

ISBN: 9781909732292

Santa Jokes

HO-HO! HO-HO-HO! HO-HO-HO!
HO-HO-HO! HO-HO-HO!

What do you get if
you cross Santa
with a duck?

A Christmas Quacker!

What says Oh, Oh, Oh?

Santa walking
backwards!

HO-HO-HO! HO-HO-HO!
HO-HO-HO! HO-HO-HO!

HO-HO! HO-HO-HO! HO-HO-HO!
-HO! HO-HO-HO! HO-HO-

What do you get if
Santa goes down the
chimney when a fire is lit?

Krisp Kringle!

What does Santa do
with fat elves?

He sends them to
an elf farm!

-HO! HO-HO-HO! HO-
HO-HO! HO-HO-HO! HO-HO

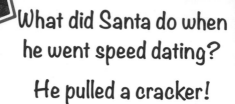

What did Santa do when he went speed dating?

He pulled a cracker!

Why don't you ever see Santa in hospital?

Because he has private elf care!

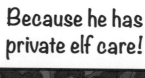

What is Santa afraid of?

The Elf and Safety Officer!

How do you know if Santa's been in your garden shed?

You've got 3 extra hoes!

Will Santa launch
an online alternative
to his usual
delivery service?

He's toying with
the idea!

What do sheep say
to Santa?

Season's bleatings!

What is 20 feet tall, has
sharp teeth and goes
Ho, Ho, Ho?

Tyranno-santa Rex!

An honest politician, a kind lawyer, and Santa were walking down the street and saw a £20 note. Which one picked it up?

Santa! The other two don't exist!

Santa's sledge broke down on Christmas Eve. He flagged down a passing motorist and asked, 'Can you help me fix my sledge?' 'Sorry', the motorist replied. 'I'm not a mechanic, I'm a chiropodist.' 'Well, can you give me a toe?'

How many chimneys
does Santa go down?

Stacks!

One time, Santa lost
his underpants...

that's how he got the
name Saint Knickerless!

HO-HO! HO-HO-HO! HO-HO-HO!
-HO! HO-HO-HO! HO-HO

What did Santa say
to Mrs. Claus when he
looked out the window?

Looks like rain, dear!

What do you call
a smelly Santa?

Farter Christmas!

-HO! HO-HO-HO! HO-HO
O-HO! HO-HO-HO! HO-HO-HO!

When Santa first passed his sleigh driving test, he came skidding down in front of the toy factory. 'Have you passed?' the elves asked.

Santa pointed proudly to the front of the sleigh...

'No-L plates!'

Santa went to the doctors with a problem...

Doctor: 'What seems to be the problem?'

Santa: 'I seem to have a mince pie stuck up my bottom!'

Doctor: 'Well, you're in luck! I've got some cream for that!'

What goes
'Ho! ho! ho! Thump!'?

Santa laughing his head off!

What goes 'Ho-squelch!
Ho-squelch! Ho-squelch!'?

Santa with snow
in his wellies!

What sort of mobile phone has Santa got?

Pay as you ho! ho! ho!!

Where does Santa stay when he's on holiday?

At a ho-ho-ho-tel!

How do you know if Santa is really a werewolf?

He has Santa claws!

What does Santa suffer from if he gets stuck in a chimney?

Claustrophobia!

Why does Santa have three gardens?

So he can 'ho, ho, ho'!

What kind of motorbike does Santa ride?

A Holly Davidson!

Present
Jokes

What is the best Christmas
present in the world?

A broken drum,
you just can't beat it!

What did the bald man
say when he got a comb
for Christmas?

Thanks, I'll never part with it!

What do you call a lobster
who won't share his
Christmas presents?

Shell-fish!

Why is a foot a good
Christmas present?

It makes a great
stocking filler!

What did the farmer get for Christmas?

A cow-culator!

What did the dog get for Christmas?

A mobile bone!

Who delivers presents to baby sharks at Christmas?

Santa Jaws!

What do wizards use
to wrap their
Christmas presents?

Spell-o-tape!

Why did Scrooge buy everyone
birds for Christmas?

Because they were
going cheap!

elf
Jokes

What do Santa's little
helpers learn at school?

The elf-abet!

How do elves greet each other?

'Small world, isn't it?'

What kind of music do
elves like best?

Wrap music!

HO-HO! HO-HO-HO! HO-HO-HO!
-HO! HO-HO-HO! HO-HO!

How do you describe
a rich elf?

Welfy!

_____

Why did Santa's helper
see the doctor?

Because he had low
'elf' esteem!

-HO! HO-HO-HO! HO-HO!
-HO! HO-HO-HO! HO-HO-HO!

How long should an elf's legs be?

Just long enough to reach the ground!

If athletes get athlete's foot, what do elves get?

Mistle-toes!

How many elves does it take to change a light bulb?

Ten! One to change the light bulb and nine to stand on each other's shoulders!

If there were eleven elves and another one came along, what would he be?

The twelf!

What do elves sing to Santa?

'Freeze a jolly good fellow'

What do you call
an elf walking
backwards?

A fle!

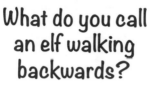

What do you call an elf
with a skin disease?

A leper-chaun!

What is a female elf called?

A shelf!

Where do you find elves?

Depends where you left them!

What do Santa's elves
do after school?

Their gnomework!

Who sings 'Blue Christmas'
and makes toy guitars?

Elfis!

Why did Santa tell
one of his elves off?

Because he was
'goblin' his dinner!

HO! HO-HO-HO! HO-HO-HO! HO-HO-HO! HO-HO-HO! H

Why did the elf put his
bed into the fireplace?

He wanted to sleep
like a log!

What do elves call it when
Father Christmas claps his
hands at the end of a play?

Santapplause!

HO-HO-HO! HO-HO-HO! HO-HO-HO! HO-HO-HO!

What does Santa do when his elves misbehave?

He gives them the sack!

Who is Santa's favourite singer?

Elf-is Presley!

Reindeer Jokes

What do reindeer hang
on their Christmas trees?

Horn-aments!

Did Rudolph go
to school?

No. He was elf-taught!

Why did no one bid for
Rudolph and Blitzen
on eBay?

Because they were
two deer!

How do you get into
Rudolph's house?

You ring the 'deer' bell!

How does Rudolph
know when Christmas
is coming?

He looks at his calen-deer!

What do reindeers have
that no other animal has?

Baby reindeer!

What do you call a reindeer
with cotton wool in his ears?

Call him anything you like,
he won't hear you!

What do you give a reindeer
with an upset tummy?

Elk-a-seltzer!

HO-HO! HO-HO-HO! HO-HO-HO! HO-HO-HO! HO-HO-HO!

What do you call a reindeer with no eyes?

No eye deer!

What do you call a reindeer with no eyes and no legs?

Still no eye deer!

HO-HO-HO! HO-HO-HO! HO-HO-HO! HO-HO-HO!

HO-HO! HO-HO-HO! HO-HO-HO!
-HO! HO-HO-HO! HO-HO

What do you call a
three-legged reindeer?

Eileen!

What game do reindeer
play in their stalls?

Stable-tennis!

HO! HO-HO-HO! HO-HO
O-HO! HO-HO-HO! HO-HO-HO!

What has antlers, pulls Santa's sleigh and is made of cement?

I don't know

A reindeer!

What about the cement?

I just threw that in to make it hard!

What would a reindeer
do if it lost it's tail?

They'd go to a 're-tail'
shop for a new one!

What's the difference between
a reindeer and a snowball?

They're both brown,
except the snowball!

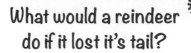

Snow Jokes

What do you get when you cross a snowman with a vampire?

Frostbite!

How do snowmen get around?

They ride an icicle!

How does a snowman
lose weight?

He stands by a radiator!

What do snowmen
have for breakfast?

Snowflakes!

What did one snowman
say to the other?

'Can you smell carrots?'

What happened when the
snowman's dog melted?

He had a slush puppy!

What is white, lives at
the North Pole and
runs around naked?

A polar bare!

What do snowmen wear
on their heads?

Ice caps!

What do snowmen
eat for lunch?

Icebergers!

Where do snowmen
go to dance?

Snowballs!

Why don't polar bears
eat penguins?

Because they can't get
the wrappers off!

What do snowmen like
on their burgers?

Chilly sauce!

What did the snowman's girlfriend give him when she was mad at him?

The cold shoulder!

What do you call a snowman in the summer?

A puddle!

What do you get when
you cross a snowman
with a baker?

Frosty the dough-man!

What do you say to
a stressed snowman?

Chill out!

Christmas Dinner Jokes

Why did the turkey
join the band?

Because it had
the drumsticks!

Who hides in the bakery
at Christmas?
A mince spy!

How does good King
Wenceslas like his pizza?

Deep pan, crisp and even!

Why did the turkey
cross the road?

To prove he wasn't chicken!

What's the most popular Christmas wine?

'I don't like Brussels sprouts!'

Why was the Brussels sprout sent to prison?

It was a repeat offender!

What do recovering chocoholics have during Christmas?

Cold turkey!

Why are there no jokes about turkey giblets?

Because the punchlines are offal!

What is the best key to get at Christmas?

A tur-key!

'Mum, can I have a dog for Christmas?'

'No, you can have turkey like everyone else!'

Who beats his chest and swings from Christmas cake to Christmas cake?

Tarzipan!

Who is never hungry at Christmas?

The turkey, he's always stuffed!

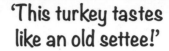

'This turkey tastes like an old settee!'

'Well, you asked for something with plenty of stuffing!'

What do you drain your carrots with at Christmas?

An Advent colander!

'We're having Grandma for Christmas dinner.'

'Really? We're having turkey!'

What do you use to make a Christmas cake?

Elf-raising flour!

Christmas Carol Jokes

How many letters are in
the Christmas alphabet?

25. There's 'No L'!

What carol is sung
in the desert?

'O Camel Ye Faithful'!

What do you get if you
cross a bell with a skunk?

'Jingle Smells'!

What do wild animals
sing at Christmas time?

'Jungle Bells, Jungle Bells,
Jungle all the way!'

What is a parent's favourite Christmas carol?

'Silent Night'!

How did Mary and Joseph know Jesus was 7lb 6oz when he was born?

They had 'A Weigh In A Manger'!

What do you call
a bunch of chess
players bragging
about their games
in a hotel lobby?

'Chess nuts boasting
in an open foyer'!

What did the Eskimos sing when they got their Christmas dinner?

'Whale meat again, don't know where, don't know when...'

What's Tarzan's favourite Christmas song?

'Jungle Bells'!

But what about his chimp?

'King Kong Merrily On High, of course'!

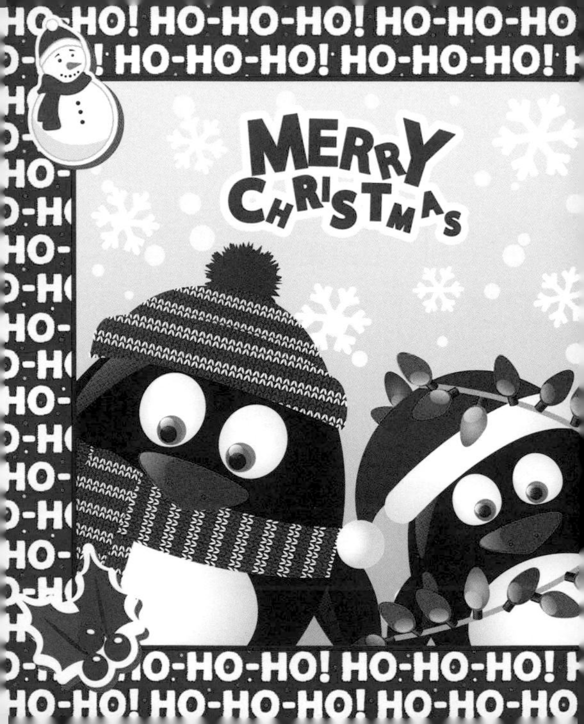
MERRY CHRISTMAS
HO-HO-HO! HO-HO-HO! HO-HO-HO!

The Rest of Christmas Jokes

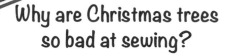

Why are Christmas trees
so bad at sewing?

They always drop
their needles!

What do you get if you eat
Christmas decorations?

Tinsilitis!

What did the beaver
say to the Christmas tree?

'Nice gnawing you'!

What's green, covered
in tinsel and goes
'ribbet, ribbet'?

Mistle-toad!

What do angry mice send to each other at Christmas?

Cross mouse cards!

How do sheep greet each other at Christmas?

Merry Christmas to ewe!

What did the stamp say to the Christmas card?

'Stick with me, we're going places'!

What squeaks and is scary?

The ghost of Christmouse past!

Knock, knock.
Who's there?
Mary.
Mary who?
Mary Christmas!

What did one angel say
to the other angel?

'Halo there'!

How do cats greet each
other at Christmas?

'A furry merry Christmas
& a happy mew year'!

HO-HO! HO-HO-HO! HO-HO-HO!
HO-HO-HO! HO-HO-HO! H

Why should you never
invite a team of footballers
for Christmas dinner?

Because they are
always dribbling!

Mary and Joseph...
now they had a
stable relationship!

HO-HO-HO! HO-HO-HO!
HO-HO! HO-HO-HO! HO-HO-HO

How did Scrooge win
the football game?

The ghost of
Christmas passed!

What's Scrooge's favourite
Christmas game?

Mean-opoly!

What happened to the man who stole an Advent calender?

He got 24 days!

What did Adam say to his wife on the day before Christmas?

'It's Christmas, Eve'!

What does the Queen call
her Christmas broadcast?

The One Show!

Why is it getting harder to
buy an Advent calender?

Because their days
are numbered!

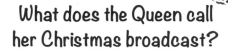

What operating system
do Advent calenders use?

Windows 24!

What kind of insect
hates Christmas?

A hum-bug!

What does Miley Cyrus have for Christmas dinner?

Twerky!

Why couldn't the skeleton go to the Christmas party?

Because he had no body to go with!

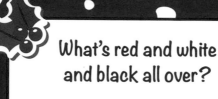

What's red and white
and black all over?

Santa coming down
the chimney!

How do you stop
a reindeer smelling?

Hold its nose!

What do vampires put on their Christmas dinner?

Grave-y!

What do you get if you cross an apple with a Christmas tree?

A pineapple!

Knock, knock.

Who's there?

Wenceslas.

Wenceslas who?

Wenceslas train home?

Knock, knock.

Who's there?

Arthur.

Arthur who?

Arthur any mince pies left?

What do ghosts have for Christmas dinner

Ghoulash!

What do you call a man wearing trousers made of Christmas wrapping paper?

Russell!